Clean Eating: 21 Day Clean Food Diet for Beginners

Start Your Weight Loss, Increase Energy, Detox, and Feel Great!

AARON PEREZ

CONTENTS

Introduction

First, I would like to begin by thanking you for purchasing this book.

In this book not only will I help you understand what Clean Eating detoxing is all about, but I will also share some recipes for the various meals you will be consuming throughout the day. As you continue with the detox plan, it will work wonders if you try your best to achieve that fabulous body you have always wished to achieve.

However, do remember that while diets work in a simple and effective manner, it is all up to you. That is, it all depends on how you maintain the balance and not just eat healthy but also indulge in a little physical activity, which you must do at least three to four times a week. If you do lead a sedentary life or your work does not involve too much physical activity, monitor your intake of calories per day. If you lead a life that is heavy in physical activity, you will need to adjust the ratio of fat to protein to carbs accordingly.

When people hear the word detox, they often only think of soups and salads, but there is a lot more to detoxing. While several people claim that diets are not the best way forward to losing weight, it is only because they tried a particular diet and failed. The reason for them failing is not the diet, but in fact it is because they don't begin the diet on the right note or are unable to maintain a balance in what they eat or drink. Hence, the diet they should have been on turns into a disaster for them! While Clean Eating detoxing does not mean you are on a diet, it only means that you are eating to rid your body of the harmful toxins after a week or two of unhealthy binge eating.

If you eat healthy and only eat the amount of food as prescribed, there will be no stopping your successful Clean Eating detox. You will not only feel lighter, but also happy!

To help you stick to your Clean Eating detox plan, you need to keep changing the food you eat, and you should feel free to do so. You can choose to eat any food that is rich in fiber and gives you an ample amount of protein, the right type, to boost your metabolic system, give you more energy, and make you more productive. With time you will be able to judge what works well for your body. Unlike a television commercial featuring a celebrity, I won't lie to you. It is a challenge to follow a regimen and stick to it without giving up on it in any way. However, I can assure you that once you make your regimen a habit for a couple of weeks or months, you will realize how much more energy you have on a daily basis. Don't believe that if you spent a few extra minutes at the gym or on your workout regimen, it gives you an all access pass to binge. No, it doesn't. Remember, the tiniest quick fixes in your routine can make a big difference to your weight loss goal.

Thanks again for purchasing this book; I do hope you enjoy the recipes I've shared!

Let's get started!

Chapter 1: The Clean Eating Detox Process

Before we begin, let's get a better understanding of what exactly is detoxification and what the process entails.

Detoxification is a process of eliminating toxins from your body through the colon, liver, glands, and nodes and can be done effectively by the human body. Sometimes, even the human body needs a little help, and this help comes when an individual consumes food, which is from fresh produce.

The detoxification process takes place when you break away from a certain kind of diet or eating habit and indulge in something that is light on the stomach and easy to digest. This way, all the collected and unwanted toxins present in the body are flushed out. While several people prefer consuming juices and salads made from fresh produce, detoxing does not mean only living on juices the whole time.

This book is meant to be a useful guide to help you stick to your Clean Eating detox plan. I've made this book as easy and straightforward as I can, and I've tried to avoid a lot of technical jargon – just the facts you need to clean up all those nasty toxins from your body in order for your system to get a boost and function smoothly.

Once you read this book, you will have done yourself a great favor. These chapters will provide you with gems of knowledge about the prime importance of juicing. You will also be provided with delicious juicing recipes, meal plans, and nutritional information that will pave the way for you to start your day right.

Remember, your mind plays an equal if not more important role than what you actually eat or drink. So, preparing yourself and your mind for what you'll experience in the next few days and weeks is extremely crucial, and research has shown that once you practice a new habit for 21 days, you are bound to remember it and carry it forward.

Similarly, in this book I share with you various recipes which will help make the detox process easy for you to follow and make it fun too, since you can get family or friends to be a part of it.

I prefer detoxing mostly after my holiday binge-eating sessions, when I know my system has been crammed with all the junk possible, and it needs a boost of energy. You will notice a change in the way you look and feel after your detox session.

On a daily basis, we read reports and watch clips on how obesity as a disease is becoming a scary phenomenon. Our bodies are fed an unhealthy range of foods, which make us heavier. Add to that the crazy lifestyles we follow, eating out has become a trend only because it is convenient for us. All the unwanted toxins fill up our body and don't have a way out. One of the ways to help your system is through detox. Just like you take time to adjust to a new workplace or a new home, similarly your body requires time to adjust to what it is being put into it. You can gradually begin juicing by adding fresh juices, fresh fruits, and vegetables to your diet during any meal. You could begin your day with a glass of fresh fruit or vegetable juice. Or you could make yourself a bottle and carry it with you to work to sip on. Juicing helps you reduce the cravings you have for unhealthy snacking and binge eating on junk food. Whenever you feel the urge to eat some fast food item as a snack, you can snack on some vegetable crudités or apple sticks with cinnamon. Juicing is different from buying juice at your nearby supermarket because unlike packaged juiced, juicing focuses on fresh produce. Juicing adds variety to your regular daily diet while helping you get the necessary nutrients from fruits and vegetables. You can make juices at home with the help of a juicer. There are several health benefits of drinking freshly juiced fruits and vegetables.

Like I mentioned previously, if we force ourselves into doing this, we are going to end up punishing our body and ourselves. If you want to lose weight in a proper manner, you have got to set your mind to it. Once you do decide and make up your mind that you want to shed those excess pounds, you have got to set yourself up emotionally. Remember, there will be no turning back, and you can trust me on the fact that you will have no regrets whatsoever once you begin.

How to Begin the Clean Eating Detox

1. Set a Date for You to Begin

Since you have decided to partake in detoxing your system, choose a month to begin wisely. Try to avoid months that have food-centric holidays in them (Thanksgiving, Christmas, etc.). Avoid months with birthdays, holidays planned, and so on. You could, of course, choose any month you fancy, but it is not a bad idea to think carefully and chalk out your plan. Deciding on a month beforehand will help provide you with inspiration.

2. Read about how you should detox before you begin

Take time out to review the specifics of the Clean Eating detox program – what you should be eating and what should not be in your pantry or refrigerator for the next 21-3o days.

3. Commit to the Program

If you have managed to comply with the two points above, you will be able to commit to the program. If you are still doubtful, however, give yourself some time. No pressure.

4. Get Your House Ready for the Program

There is no better way to follow the program and succeed than to plan and prepare. Consider it a battle you are fighting for your own health. Clean out your pantry, and those snack and treat-filled cupboards. Stock your kitchen with the essentials you require for the next 21 days. Avoid sneaking in anything, which will be a deterrent in your way.

5. Plan for Success

There will be days when you are bound to find yourself in a difficult situation. Create a plan that will help you handle those events with ease. Remember, it is better to face your fears than run back to square one.

The guidelines I will now share with you are what you will be following for the next 30 days. The rules will not only help you understand what is expected of you in the next 30 days, but will also help you make better food choices.

I need you to take a vow to follow these rules and at least make the effort not to indulge in any form of cheats.

Food Items to be Avoided

- **Sugar**

  Stevia, yacon, and coconut honey are okay, but any other kind of sugar, like agave nectar or sugar in processed food items etc., is a strict no-no. Look up articles on how to read labels. Sugar is in most products you buy at the supermarket.

- **Alcohol**

  No consuming wine, tequila, beer, etc. in any form or include them as ingredients while cooking.

- **Grains**

This again requires you to read the labels on the products you purchase. Wheat, rye, barley, oats, millet, and all gluten-free pseudo cereals like amaranth, buckwheat, or quinoa.

- **Carrageenan, MSG**

    These ingredients should not appear in any form on the ingredient list of your processed food or beverage.

- **Baked Goods or Junk Food with the Approved Ingredients**

    No coconut cream or apple strudel. Your cravings will not subside, and you will find it even more difficult to change and control your eating habits, even if the particular food items are made with ingredients that are allowed during the Clean Eating detox program.

- **Junk the Weighing Scale and the Measuring Tape**

  No analyzing body fat, weighing yourself, or bringing out the tape measure during this program. If you focus on weighing yourself before and after the program, you will miss all the benefits you could receive from this program. So go ahead, toss that scale into the garbage bag.

Before you begin the detox clean eating program, you will have to initiate your body through the pre-cleansing phase. You can begin this phase 3 days before the actual start of the detox plan.

Similarly, after you are done with the pre-cleansing phase

and the 21 day clean detox program, you need to gradually

re-initiate the avoided food items into your system. The re-

initiation phase usually takes about 5-7 days.

Chapter 2: Clean Eating 21 Days Recipes

Recipe 1: Avocado Salsa with Salmon

Serves – 4-6

Prep Time – 10 minutes

Cook Time – 15 minutes

Wild caught salmon is the perfect choice for this recipe. The avocado salsa pairs beautifully with the salmon, making this dish work perfectly.

Ingredients

2 Fillets Salmon

1 teaspoon cumin

1 teaspoon paprika

1-2 tablespoons of clarified butter

A pinch of black pepper powder

A pinch of sea salt

For the Salsa

1 medium avocado, peeled, cored and chopped

1 large red onion, finely chopped

2 jalapeno peppers, de-seeded, finely chopped

4-5 tablespoons of freshly squeezed Lemon Juice

Handful of Fresh Cilantro, finely chopped

Method:

To make the salsa, take a large mixing bowl, and combine all the salsa ingredients and give it a good mix. Place this salsa mixture in the fridge until you are ready to serve.

Pre-heat your oven to 400 degrees Fahrenheit. Place the salmon on a lightly greased baking tray. Mix all the spices in a bowl, and gently apply all over the salmon. Add a little bit of clarified butter in the baking pan, and place the salmon on it. Bake the fish for 12-15 minutes until the salmon is tender and flakes easily with a fork. Serve with the chilled avocado salsa.

Recipe 2: Multi-Color Salad

Serves – 1

Prep Time – 15 minutes

Cook Time – Nil

This salad is packed with fiber, vitamins like C and A, and will surely make your 21 day meal plan very colorful and nutritious. The romaine lettuce has a high water content that keeps the body hydrated for a good amount of time, whereas the red cabbage and carrots are rich in fiber that aids in healthy digestion.

Ingredients

1 ½ cups of grated purple cabbage

2 medium carrots, cut into juliennes

1 ½ cups of grated romaine lettuce

1/2 cup tahini dressing (recipe below)

For dressing:

4 tablespoons of raw tahini paste

2 tablespoons of olive oil

4 tablespoons of freshly squeezed lemon juice

1 teaspoon sea salt

Method

Take a blender, and puree all the ingredients for the salad dressing together until very smooth. Keep 1/2 cup of the dressing for your salad aside, and store the remaining in a glass jar for later use (you can store it in the refrigerator for up to three days). In a large mixing bowl, add the grated cabbage, lettuce, carrots and toss the salad dressing, and serve immediately. To serve this as a main course, add avocado or roasted chicken to the salad, and serve.

Recipe 3: Buffalo Ranch and Peppers

Serves – 4

Prep Time – 20 minutes

Cooking Time – 20 minutes

This recipe is great, as it shows you how to make your own ranch dressing, thereby completely cutting off the added MSG and other artificial additives.

Ingredients

4 chicken breasts

1 medium onion, sliced

½ teaspoon dried parsley

½ teaspoon dried dill

½ teaspoon dried chives

½ teaspoon garlic powder

½ teaspoon onion powder

A pinch of sea salt

½ teaspoon of black pepper

3-4 tablespoon of clarified butter for greasing and baking

2 peppers, diced

4 tablespoons of hot sauce

Guacamole

2 avocados, peeled, cored and pulped

1 jalapeno, de-seeded, and minced

1 small red onion, finely chopped

3 tablespoons of cilantro, finely chopped

1 tablespoon of lime, juiced

Sea salt, as needed

Method

First of all preheat your oven to 350 degrees. In the meanwhile, mix your dried spices together in a mixing bowl. Then, place the chicken breasts, diced peppers and sliced onions on a greased baking tray and sprinkle the dried spices over it. Next, sprinkle the salt and pepper over the peppers, onions and chicken breasts. Next, add a small amount of clarified butter on each of the chicken breasts and bake it for 25-30 minutes or until chicken is cooked through. While the chicken is baking in the oven, prepare the sauce and the guacamole. To make the sauce, melt ¼-cup butter in a saucepan over medium low heat. Once it has melted, pour in the hot sauce and stir well. To make the guacamole, just all all the ingredients for the guacamole in a blender and whip it up till you get a smooth, creamy paste and set aside. Once the chicken is baked, cut it into bite size pieces and place on a platter. Pour the hot sauce mixture over the chicken bits, onions, and peppers and serve with guacamole.

Recipe 4: Detox Beef Carne

Serves- 2-3

Prep Time – 1 – 24 hours

Cooking Time – 25 minutes

This is probably the best way to eat steak. It is so flavorful and so tender and juicy. You can make the marinade the night before, and then it only takes minutes to cook the steak when you need it. You can also sauté a bunch of vegetables.

Ingredients

3 lbs Steak, 1 inch thick

1/2 cup white vinegar

1/2 cup coconut oil

Juice of 1 lime

3 cloves of garlic, minced

Salt as needed

1-teaspoon pepper powder

1-teaspoon chili powder

1-teaspoon garlic powder

1-teaspoon cumin powder

1 teaspoon dried oregano

1 teaspoon smoked paprika

Method

In a large mixing bowl, combine the white vinegar, olive oil, limejuice, garlic, and spices, and give it a good mix. Pour this marinade over the steak placed in another bowl, and coat it well. Keep this in the fridge for a couple of hours. Once it has marinated well, set the oven to broil, and place the rack on the top position.

Then, broil the marinated steak for 6-7 minutes, flip it over, and broil it for 5 more minutes on medium. Let it rest for 10 minutes, and cut it steak into thin slices and serve with the avocado salsa and lime wedges, topped with fresh cilantro.

Recipe 5: One Pot Balsamic Beef Roast

Serves – 6-8

Prep Time – 15 minutes

Cooking Time – 25-30 minutes

This meal only takes minutes to prepare, and the slow cooker does all the work for you. This can be served alongside baked sweet potatoes, cooked greens, and cauliflower mash for an ultimate comfort food meal. Balsamic vinegar adds a nice depth of flavor to this dish.

Ingredients

3 lbs roast beef

1 large red onion, diced

½ cup balsamic vinegar

2 teaspoons of minced garlic

1-cup chicken broth (can use beef stock as well)

2-3 tablespoons of coconut aminos

½ teaspoon of red pepper, flakes or minced

Sea salt as needed

½ teaspoon of black pepper

Method

The first thing to do is to place your entire roast beef in a crock-pot, with the fat side facing down. Next, add all the other ingredients on the roast. Then sprinkle some salt and pepper on top of the roast. Cover the beef and, cook on low flame for at least 7-8 hours. The meat is done when it is browned on top and shreds easily with the help of a fork. Once the meat is cooked, remove it from the crock-pot, and place it on a platter. Pour the remaining ingredients from the crock-pot into a blender, and whir it up till you get gravy like consistency. Pour this gravy in a bowl, and serve it with the roast beef. Sprinkle some chopped chives, cilantro, or parsley on top if needed.

Recipe 6: Pancetta Sweet Potato Hash

Serves – 2-3

Prep Time – 10 minutes

Cook Time – 15 minutes

This dish is great for a breakfast you would like to share with your whole family, and it does not take long to prepare and cook.

Ingredients

2 sweet potatoes, finely shredded

2 shallots, roughly chopped

4-5 cloves of garlic, minced

½ teaspoon of sea salt

4 ounces pancetta

2 slices thick-cut bacon, chopped into small bite-sized pieces

Method

First, place a pan over medium-high heat. Once the pan is heated, add the bits of bacon and pancetta, and cook it for 5 minutes or until crispy. Flip the pieces over occasionally, using a spoon or spatula. Once the bacon and pancetta are cooked, remove them from the pan and place them on a paper-towel. Then, throw in the shallots and garlic in the same pan and cook them for a minute, then add the potatoes, and cook for a few more minutes. Add the sea salt, and stir it with a wooden spoon every few minutes until they are cooked through, but not overcooked. Once the potatoes are cooked, remove the pan from the heat, and mix in about ¾ of the bacon bits and pancetta and place it in a serving dish. Use the rest of the bacon bits and

pancetta for garnishing. Additionally, you can also serve

with boiled or fried eggs and/or avocado on top.

Recipe 7: Healthy Butter Chicken

Serves – 4-6

Prep Time – 1 – 24 hours

Cooking Time – 25 minutes

Ideally, and if time permits, you should marinate the chicken overnight in a mixture of lemon juice, garlic, salt, and garam masala. If you cannot do it overnight, try to give it at least a couple of hours. The lemon juice will start to denature the protein in the meat, making that chicken juicier and tender, while the salt will really get into the meat, rendering it tastier.

When you are ready to cook your chicken, rinse it under cold running water, and then pat it until it is completely dry.

Ingredients

4 large chicken breasts, cut into 1" to 2" pieces

1/2 cup freshly squeezed lemon juice

2 cloves of garlic, minced

1-tablespoon Himalayan salt

1-tablespoon garam masala

1/4 cup clarified butter

1 large onion, diced

2 tablespoons fresh ginger, minced

1-tablespoon ras el hanout

1-teaspoon ground Ceylon cinnamon

1/2-teaspoon chipotle powder

1/4 teaspoon ground white pepper

1 large can (28 oz/798 ml) of crushed tomatoes

2 cups of water

2 tablespoons date paste

1/2-cup full fat coconut milk

1/2 cup of almond butter

227g mushrooms cut in half

227g fresh spinach, washed and chopped

Method

For this recipe, it is ideal to marinate the chicken overnight in lemon juice, garlic, salt, and garam masala. Once the chicken has marinated well, melt some clarified butter in a large skillet set over medium-high flame and add the marinated chicken pieces into it. Cook the chicken for about 5-6 minutes until it is nice and golden brown on all sides. Place the golden brown chicken in a bowl along with its juices. In the same skillet, add the onion, garlic, and ginger and cook for 3-4 minutes, until the vegetables are tender and begin to brown slightly. At this stage, add the chicken back to the skillet, add in the garam masala, ras el hanout, cinnamon powder, chipotle powder, and white pepper, and mix it well. Next, pour the crushed tomatoes, date paste, and water, and let it simmer for half an hour. In the meantime, take a mixing bowl, and whisk together the coconut milk and almond butter until well combined. Add this mixture to the chicken, stir well, and cook for 5 minutes. While the chicken is simmering, take another pan and brown the mushrooms, and add it to the chicken. Add the spinach too, mix it well, and then cook it until the spinach has wilted; serve.

Recipe 8: Beef with Potatoes

Serves – 4

Prep Time – 15 minutes

Cooking Time – 20-25 minutes

One of the best things about this dish is it that it is so flavorful, and cooked in just one skillet: less utensils to be washed!

Ingredients

2 tablespoons of Ghee

1 large Vidalia onion, chopped

4 carrots, peeled, finely chopped

$1/4$-teaspoon allspice powder

1-2 pinches of clove powder

⅛ teaspoon cinnamon powder

¼-teaspoon ground thyme

¾-teaspoon ground mustard

¼-teaspoon black pepper powder

¼ teaspoon rubbed sage

5 cloves of garlic, chopped

1½ lbs Yukon potatoes, chopped

1 cup chicken stock

1¾ tsp salt, divided

1 lb ground lean beef

Method

Place a skillet over medium heat, and add the clarified butter to it. Then, add the onions, carrots, and seasonings with a pinch of the salt, and mix it well. Cook this mixture until the onions turn translucent and then add the garlic and cook for a minute more. Next, add the chicken stock, chopped potatoes, and some salt if using unsalted chicken stock, and bring to a boil, and let it simmer. Cover the pan with a lid, and let it cook for 5 more minutes by stirring it occasionally. Remove the lid, and let the stock reduce. At this stage add the beef and the remaining salt, and cook it till the beef crumbles. In case the potatoes are uncooked but the beef is done, just add some more chicken stock (or water), and boil until the potatoes are tender.

Recipe 9: Almond, Date and Banana Smoothie

Serves – 3

Prep Time – 15 minutes

Cooking Time – 20-25 minutes

This almond date banana smoothie is naturally sweet and has a character all its own. A frozen banana composes the base, a spoonful of almond butter adds a nutty tone, and a handful of dates give it a rounded flavor. Small pieces of date are left in the drink, giving a nice little treat for each bite. Though this smoothie may be simple, the flavors are sophisticated and perfect for an early morning or afternoon on the go.

Ingredients

1 large frozen banana

4-5 dried pitted dates

1 tablespoon Almond butter

1 teaspoon ground flax seeds

¾ cup coconut milk

Method

Place all the ingredients in a blender, and blend until smooth. Pour into a glass, and serve immediately.

Recipe 10: Salmon and Dill Pockets

Serves – 2

Prep Time – 5 minutes

Cooking Time – 20 minutes

This dish is quick and easy to make. It is a simple flavor packed dish.

Ingredients

1 sheet of tin foil

2 pieces of salmon

3-4 tablespoons of lemon juice

2 cloves garlic, minced

2 teaspoons of dill

5 tablespoons of butter, divided

1 teaspoon old bay seasoning

A handful of asparagus, trimmed

Method

First, start by preheating the oven to 400 degrees. While that is happening, melt 2 tablespoons of butter, garlic, dill, and lemon juice in the microwave. Next, place the asparagus on the tin foil, top it with the remaining butter, place the salmon filet on top, and brush the herbed butter garlic mixture over it. Carefully, close the sides of the tin foil, and bake the salmon pockets at 400 for 20 minutes. Once done, remove the fish from the foil, transfer it onto a plate, and serve.

Recipe 11: The Ultimate Morning Juice

Serves – 2

Prep Time – 5 minutes

Cooking Time – 20 minutes

In this juice we use cranberries along with ginger and pomegranate. Cranberries are one of the healthiest fruits of all as they are packed with antioxidants and also rich in other vital nutrients required for good health. Cranberries are known to improve the immune function and also lowers the risk of UTI's. in addition, this "super food" is also rich in other vitamins, low in calories and assists in weight loss too!

Ingredients

1 large pomegranate,

1 inch piece of g

1 cup of Fresh cranberries

2-3 cubes of crushed ice

Method

In a juicer or blender, add all the fruits and the ginger. Blend for a few minutes until it all comes together. Top up your glass with crushed ice. Pour the juice over it and enjoy it fresh.

Recipe 12: Apple, Pomegranate Juice

Serves – 2

Prep Time – 5 minutes

Cooking Time – 20 minutes

This juice is an easy recipe that helps give you a quick boost of energy, especially during summer when you get drained out of energy quite easily. Pomegranate is a good source of vitamin C and vitamin K. There is no need to add any sugar or sweetener to this juice. Using apples helps boost the sweetness in this juice.

Ingredients

2 large apples, peeled, cored and chopped

2 large pomegranates, peeled and seeded

3-4 ice cubes

Method

Add the fruits into a blender, and blend it on high till they're mixed well. Next, add the ice cubes and blend again for a minute more till you get an even consistency. Pour into a tall glass, and enjoy!

Recipe 13: Tropical Sunrise Juice

Serves – 2

Prep Time – 5 minutes

Cooking Time – 15 minutes

A brilliant blend of delicious fruits to keep you refreshed on a hot summer day.

Ingredients

10 strawberries

3 peaches, cored

1 pear, chopped

1 mango, chopped

½ inch piece of ginger

Method

Add all the ingredients into a juicer, and blend it on high for a few minutes until the ingredients are mixed well. Pour and serve in a glass with ice.

Recipe 14: Crazy Berry Shots

Serves – 2

Prep Time – 5 minutes

Cooking Time – 10 minutes

This smooth, rich berry deliciousness tastes like summer in a glass. The blackberries, blueberries, strawberries, and raspberries combine perfectly to create the perfect balance of juicy flavors. This juice also gives you the most intense intake of raw vitamins, minerals, enzymes and antioxidants all of which help to cleanse and restore the body.

Ingredients

2 apples

1 cucumber

½ cup of blueberries

½ cup of strawberries

½ cup of raspberries

½ cup of blackberries

Method

Place all the ingredients in the juicer, and blend it on high for a few minutes till a rich, creamy consistency is achieved. Pour in a glass, and serve chilled.

Recipe 15: Mango Mayhem

Serves – 2

Prep Time – 5 minutes

Cooking Time – 10 minutes

This juice cleanse recipe of oranges, carrots, and mangoes is great for energy! Mangoes are great for digestion, skin care, memory and concentration. Carrots and Oranges contain antioxidants and help with anti aging. All three ingredients are great for heart disease as well.

Ingredients

5 carrots, peeled and chopped

2 oranges, peeled

1 mango, peeled and roughly chopped

Method

Add the mangoes, carrots, and oranges into a juicer, and blend it till a thick, juice is attained. Pour into a glass, add ice cubes (optional), and serve.

Conclusion

As the 21-day program ends, you will notice several changes and the difference you have made for your body. To help you recap some of the key points:

1. Eating with very strict rules is easier than practicing moderation.

2. Nothing about the Clean Eating 21 Days Diet is restrictive.

3. Food is how we bond with other people, and it helps you understand your relationship between food and your body.

4. You will learn to listen to your body and eat only when you are hungry and not out of emotion or on an impulse.

5. You will learn about how your body reacts to certain food

6. Regular meals are good for you.

7. Sugar is not your friend.

8. You will discover some great flavor combinations

9. Cooking whole foods is easy

10. Breakfast is always the most important meal.

On the whole, this 21-day cleansing program helps you to change your views on food and helps you to make better food choices that are not only healthy, but tasty too! So, hope you enjoy your 21-day diet regime with the delicious recipes given above. Happy eating!

- Aaron Perez

Made in the USA
Middletown, DE
05 April 2018